THE POWER OF STAGING

A SELLER'S GUIDE TO HOME STAGING

ANDY CAPELLUTO

CONTENTS

Hi, I am Andy Capelluto, founder and CEO of the International School of Staging. In 2004, I created and launched the very first online home staging course. Since then, several thousand real estate agents and home stagers have taken my live and online classes on The Power of Staging®

As an interior designer, who has sold many homes around the world, I quickly realized that a home that looks spectacular and is priced right, sells quickly. My last home sold in seven hours and significantly exceeded the asking price in a market where homes weren't selling so fast.

As a home stager, I've spent many hours evaluating both the exterior and interior of houses and doing detailed consultations for sellers, making suggestions on how best to present their homes for the real estate market.

This book was created to guide you through the process as you prepare your home for the real estate market. I'd like to work with you and share some of the formulas, skills, tips and tricks of the trade that I've developed over many years in the industry.

Home staging is not interior design or interior decorating. Home staging is the process of preparing a home for sale using proven techniques that involve making relatively quick and cost-effective modifications to a house so that it appeals to a wider audience and stands out in the marketplace.

Right now, I'd like to give you some guidance as to how and where to begin. But first, let me draw an analogy that everyone can relate to.

Think back to the first sight you saw this morning when you woke up and stumbled to the bathroom mirror. Now think of yourself at an important event – your prom, your wedding, even a job interview. How much behind–the-scenes work did you put into dressing for your high school reunion?

We have showered, shaved, sprayed, primed and painted, and finally we have adorned ourselves with a presentable outfit and a few sparkling accessories. In the end, we look quite different from the person we saw in the bathroom mirror this morning.

Putting a home on the market is pretty much the same process. It involves hours of preparation for the final presentation. This is the essence of home staging.

Home staging is no longer a buzzword, but a mainstream concept that has changed the way residential listings are sold. Today's buyers are busier, pickier and savvier than ever before.

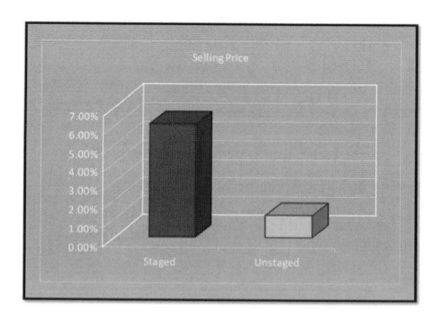

Statistics prove over and over again that homes that are priced right and are move-in ready, sell quickly.

The principles of staging are simple and straightforward:

1. To present a clean, tidy house that is in a good state of repair

2. To accentuate the positive features and minimize the negatives

3. To create a fantasy for the prospective buyer

The interesting thing about home staging is that the formula remains the same for any size, style or price point of home, anywhere in the world.

Every staging consultation begins at the entrance to the property, as I evaluate the exterior with a view to creating fabulous curb appeal. I place emphasis on the front door to ensure that the area looks clean and inviting. Working my way through the interior of the home, I go room by room, assessing where improvements can be made.

Let me take you through the process, step by step.

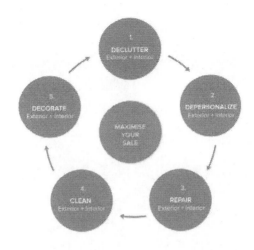

There are 5 important steps to staging a home. In order to organize and prepare for the sale and your move we recommend that these 5 important steps happen in this exact order ...

Before   After

First step, we DECLUTTER.

Then we DEPERSONALIZE.

The next step is to REPAIR, which includes updating and upgrading.

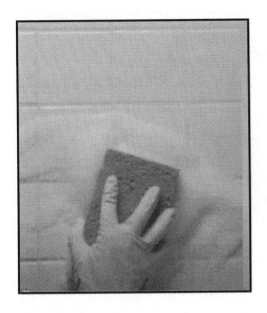

Following that, we CLEAN,

Before   After

and then finally we DECORATE.
Over the next several sections, I'm going to walk you through what needs to
be done in each of these steps so that you can maximize the sale of your
home when it hits the market.

INTERNATIONAL

SCHOOL OF STAGING

STEP 1: DECLUTTER

Step 1 begins where I take you through an efficient way to DECLUTTER your home.

Before   After

Remember, it's important to make a great first impression when listing your home for the real estate market. By preparing for the sale and upcoming move in an organized way, your home will look fabulous, sell quickly and bring in top dollar.

Decluttering is the most important action you can take in preparing a home for the real estate market. Your goal is to remove all visible clutter and turn disorder into order.

For the exterior of the home, decluttering would involve cutting back overgrowth like tree branches that are touching the gutters or the roof of the home,

removing weeds, raking leaves and mowing the lawn,

or shoveling a clear pathway through the snow, if you've had a recent snowfall. A great idea would be to have a gardening team do a thorough cleanup of the yard and then remove all the yard waste.

Before   After

Indoors, decluttering would involve removing any excess items and unnecessary furniture and accessories, which will instantly make rooms look bigger. Remove all unnecessary items that take up precious floor space, like ottomans, small tables and small rugs.

Before
After

Clutter and disorganization make people feel ill at ease, so when staging a home we want to see tidy areas, and empty floor space rather than lots of stuff.

Clutter creates the impression that a house is too small and that it lacks sufficient storage. Don't even think of hiding the clutter in closets, as people will open them to see what space they will have available to them, so tidy and minimize the contents of closets as well. If it's smaller than the palm of your hand, it's clutter.

WE RECOMMEND THE 'FIVE-PILE PROCESS'

This will help you to get organized for your upcoming move. It involves going room by room and separating the contents of each room into five piles. Remember that getting rid of superfluous items at this stage will make moving both less expensive (less volume) and more satisfying when you unpack your belongings in your new home. The ultimate goal in staging is for you to display only those items that enhance the home.

Divide the contents of each room into the following five piles:

<u>Pile # 1:</u> Items to throw out – This is trash, so why take it to your new home?

Pile # 2: Items to recycle – Let's dispose of any waste responsibly.

<u>Pile # 3</u>: Items to donate – Find a charity that will pick up your donation.

Pile # 4: Items to pack up in a box ready for your new home – Keep only what you love and need for your new home.

<u>Pile # 5</u>: Items to keep and display – Use these as staging accessories.

Decluttering the bathrooms

Before   After

The seller should completely remove all items, and store out of sight everything from the countertops. In bathrooms, that means all soap scraps, washcloths, toothpaste, toothbrushes, cosmetics and hair accessories. Remove kids' bath toys and other assistive devices.

Your items for daily use should be kept in a container under the sink, which would make it quick and easy to store when house hunters come to view the home.

Decluttering the kitchen

Before

After

Before   After

The same goes for the kitchen. Remove sponges, dirty dishcloths, pot scrubbers and cleaning liquids. If you're using the tops of your kitchen cabinets to display or store items, we recommend that you remove those as well.

Decluttering the living room

Remove small furnishings, little rugs, dying plants and any additional accessories that take up space. Declutter and organize book shelves as well.

Decluttering the dining room

Remove overly large furniture pieces. Minimize the number of chairs and position them as close to the table as possible, thereby keeping the space in the dining room open.

Reduce the contents of the china cabinet by displaying one bold piece per window.

Decluttering the bedrooms

Before

After

Reduce the contents of the bedroom. The bed is the focal point and the most important piece of furniture.

Before After

Think of a hotel room: all you need is a beautifully made bed, bedside table, bedside lamp, dresser and perhaps a chair. Professional organizers are available to assist people who hoard.

Decluttering the garage

Eliminate and organize the contents of the garage. Responsibly dispose of paint, fertilizers and other chemicals. Tidy and reduce the contents of the garage so that it has space for cars.

Pest control products could indicate to prospective buyers that you have a pest or rodent problem.

Moving advice

Time your move right

Movers charge more on weekends, as well as at the beginning and the end of the month; try to schedule your move on a Tuesday or Wednesday in the middle of the month. Any company you use should be licensed, bonded, experienced and recommended. Always read the fine print.

There is a new trend in companies that will deliver a storage container to your home and allow you to pack it at your leisure. They will then deliver it to your new address thereby saving you some moving costs. The container should be removed from the property prior to taking professional listing photographs.

There is always the less expensive but also less preferable option of storing excess items in boxes stacked neatly in the basement or garage. We emphasize that the items be properly boxed and stacked in a way that prospective buyers are able to see the perimeter of the room where the boxes are being stored.

Before   After

And so you're off to a great start having removed the excess from your home. Now let's focus on the next step in the home staging process, which is all about **DEPERSONALIZING**.

Refer to **DECLUTTER CHECKLIST** at the end of the book.

STEP 2: DEPERSONALIZE

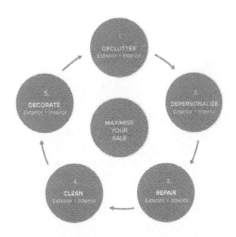

Decluttering is the foundation of the home staging process, and in this section we look at the second step, DEPERSONALIZE. This step is of equal importance as you prepare your home for the sale with the understanding that strangers will be walking through your property. To remove and safeguard your personal property it's best to take evidence of your family out of the home.

When depersonalizing the exterior of the home, we strongly suggest removing items like RV's, boats, motorbikes and extra vehicles that would detract from the view of the home.

Likewise, we should minimize collections of garden ornaments like gnomes, fairies and garden signs. Children's outdoor toys should be tidied and dog kennels, animal cages

and yard waste bins placed in an area where they are out of view of the home.

Remove old wreaths from the front door and keep both outdoor and indoor holiday decorations to a stylish minimum.

Indoors you want to remove everything that provides any personal information about the people who live in the home.

This means removing all photographs and clearing off all information from bulletin boards, such as kid's schedules and invitations. These only serve as a distraction, and you don't want to lose a naturally curious prospective buyer to a display of family photographs. A good place to start is the refrigerator with all those magnets and papers that get stuck on it.

Most importantly you don't want people coming through your home and finding personal information that could be used for any number of unscrupulous actions. It is important to protect your privacy.

As you go through your home organizing, discarding and packing, ask yourself:

Is this item valuable to me?

Is this information personal and can it be used against me or members of my family by someone with ill intent?

Is this item personal or dangerous if it falls into the wrong hands?

If so, remove it for safe-keeping or lock it away !

Could any item, artifact or aroma in your home upset people's sensitivities? For example cultural artifacts, chemicals, perfumes or other odors.

Here too you continue organizing your belongings using the Five-pile Process:

1. Items to throw out

2. Items to recycle

3. Items to donate

4. Items to keep and display

5. Items to pack up in a box ready for your new home

LOCK AWAY OR REMOVE THESE ITEMS FROM YOUR HOME

Family photographs

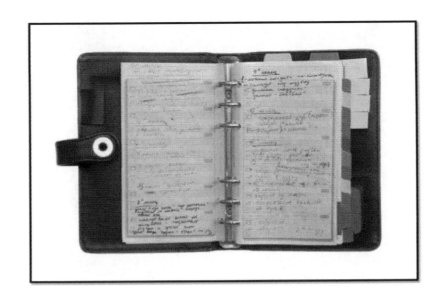

Family calendar and message boards

Information on the bulletin board

Refrigerator magnets

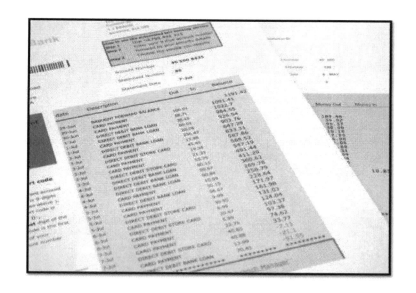

Bank and credit card statements

Pin numbers and security codes

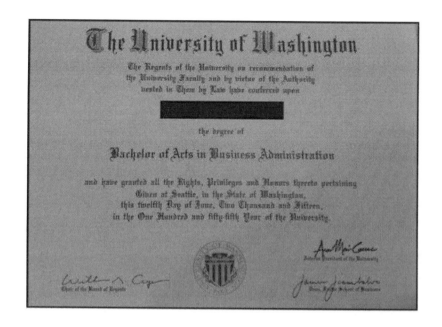

Diplomas, awards, certificates

Sports trophies

House and car keys

Weapons

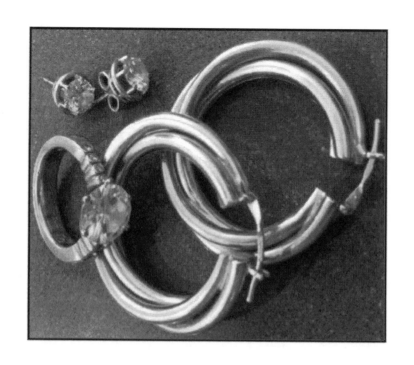

Expensive jewelry

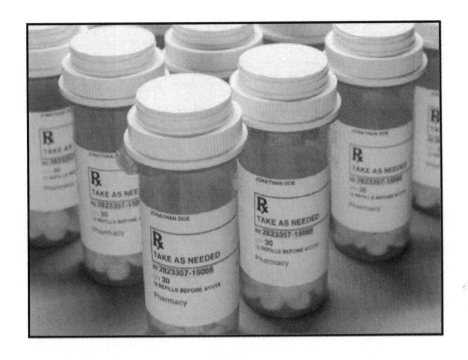

Prescription drugs

Religious items

Flags of foreign countries

Hunting memorabilia

Expensive art objects

Risqué art

Adult literature & personal items

Political literature

Pets, cages and crates

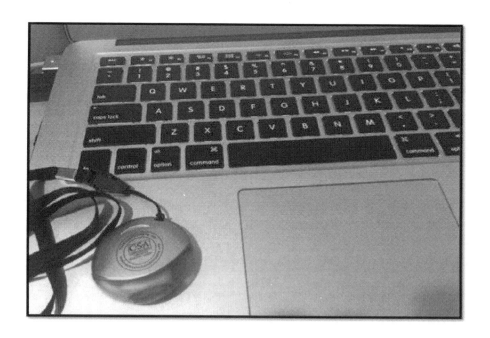

Laptops, iPads, mobile phones

Potpourri, perfumed plugins, scented candles

Pet droppings

Throughout the home prepping process, you will come across items that should be either locked away or removed from the home for safekeeping.

Recently I heard of a lady who had an expensive bottle of perfume stolen from their open house. An open house is an open invitation for anyone and everyone to come into your personal space. Keep that in mind as you 'stranger proof' and depersonalize your property.

Refer to the **DEPERSONALISE CHECKLIST** at the end of the book.

Having completed these first two important steps, you're hopefully feeling empowered and organized.

Most important of all we have removed 'the family' from the home. The next section is equally as important: presenting a home that is updated, upgraded and in a good state of **REPAIR**.

INTERNATIONAL
SCHOOL OF STAGING

STEP 3: REPAIR

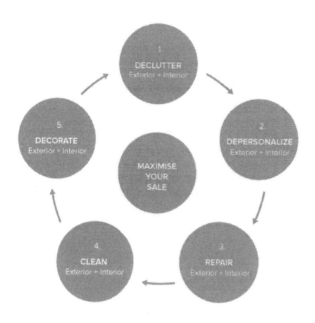

Now that you've decluttered and depersonalized, the next part of the process is to REPAIR.

This involves updating, upgrading and replacing as much as you possibly can.

This is an important step because when a home is in a good state of repair it indicates to house hunters that it had been well maintained.

This is a magnet for prospective buyers. They might think twice about 'nickel & diming' you, and submitting 'lowball' offers.

Replace the mailbox if necessary and ensure that the house numbers are clearly visible.

Before   After

Outdoor area repairs would include maintenance and painting of decks and fences.

Before After

Make sure that water features are in good working order and the swimming pool filter and pump are working properly.

Update old and tired outdoor furniture with a coat of paint.

Before   After

Replacing sod if your lawn is full of dead patches or overrun with weeds would be another worthwhile update.

Special emphasis should be placed on the front door area. Create a focal point of the front door by painting it a cheerful color, using an exterior non-glossy paint. Get inspiration from decorating magazines and brainstorm with your agent or a friend as to which color would be best.

It's always a good idea to replace the front door mat and to polish or if necessary replace the front door hardware.

Before   After

There is a wide range of opportunities to spend your staging dollars, and much depends on your budget and the condition of your home. There is no need to feel overwhelmed or under pressure to do it all. I suggest you prioritize and focus your attention on what the eye can see, for example:

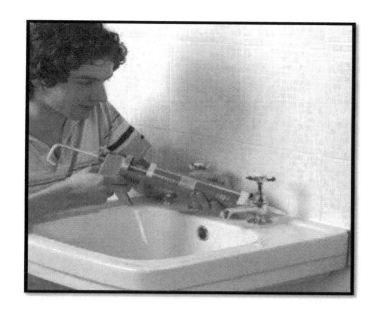

leaking faucets, grimy caulking, broken tiles and tarnished bathroom hardware.

Replacing shower curtains, drawer pulls and light bulbs are inexpensive and visible upgrades.

Replacing old worn carpeting and dated light fixtures are upgrades that will pay for themselves.

Ensure that all doors especially those on runners, work properly and are squeak free.

Painting is the cheapest, fastest most impactful upgrade you can make when selling a home. Hardware and paint stores are staffed with experts to guide you through the process. Avoid selecting anything other than a light neutral color. Resist the urge to paint interior accent colors. Let the new homeowners select their own accent colors if desired.

Before   After

It's best to present a light colored and bright clean canvas onto which the new owners can add their personalities.

Remember to never select a paint color from a tiny paint swatch. Rather test the paint color on a section on the wall. Paint companies sell sample quantities of paint colors. Fill any holes left behind in the walls with spackling.

Before   After

Old-fashioned wood paneling can be easily updated by painting with a light neutral color. This will leave them with a brighter, fresher and more modern look. Here again, I strongly advise consulting with experts at a hardware or paint store for guidance.

Refinishing or laying hardwood floors will add to the final asking price of a home. Avoid a high gloss finish as it's highly toxic and looks overly shiny. A matte finish is preferable.

Before · After

We don't recommend undertaking any major remodeling projects; leave that up to the new homeowners to upgrade their new home according to their needs.

If you are thinking about replacing appliances, the trend is toward stainless steel. This would be an investment that would pay for itself.

Our approach to staging the kitchen and bathrooms is always the same. Take a long, hard critical look at the room, surface by surface. Check out the condition of the six walls, which includes the ceiling, four walls and floor.

Look at the condition and appearance of the bathtub, sinks and countertops. Specifically, check the caulking around the edge of the bathtub and sinks. Soap scum, mold and old caulking are most unsightly.

It is fairly simple to remove the old caulking using a small plastic scraper made specifically for this job. Then clean the area well and replace using silicone caulking in either clear or white.

Either you or your handyman could tackle this job with ease, making for an effective low-cost improvement. It is important to repair any leaking or dripping faucets, not just in the bathrooms but anywhere inside and outside the house.

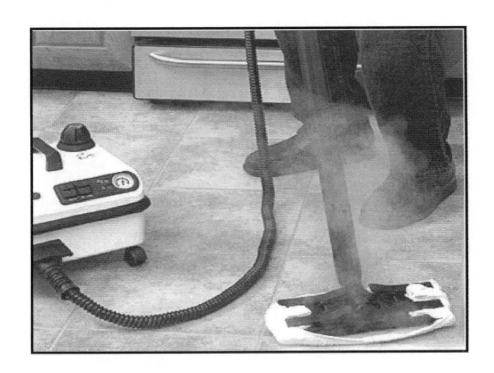

Professional steam cleaning of tiles and grout always achieves great results.

Remove dated wallpaper especially wallpaper borders. There are a number of methods you can use, steaming being the most earth-friendly. Although the quickest, easiest method is to simply paint over wallpaper, with time budget and energy permitting, removing wallpaper is preferable to painting over it. Following this update with a coat of neutral paint would immediately modernize and freshen up the appearance of a room. I advise against applying new wallpaper in an effort to improve the look of any room.

Refer to the **<u>REPAIR CHECKLIST</u>** at the end of the book.

This section will have your home updated, upgraded and REPAIRED. With all the work you've completed, I imagine your house is starting to look pretty good. But wait, a vital step is yet to be tackled.

The next step is an imperative one. Showcasing a spotlessly **CLEAN** home.

INTERNATIONAL
SCHOOL OF STAGING

STEP 4: CLEAN

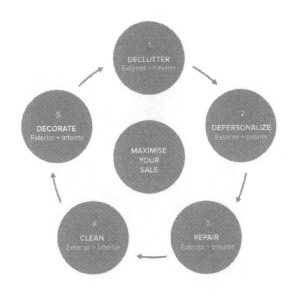

Welcome to the fourth and undeniably essential step you should take when preparing your home for the real estate market: CLEANING. We've covered the groundwork for showing your home in its best possible light, and now it's time to clean it until it sparkles.

Presenting a home that is move-in ready means that the new owners can move right in, unpack their belongings and get on with their busy lives. No one wants to move into a new home and spend days cleaning out other people's dirt and grime.

Before

After

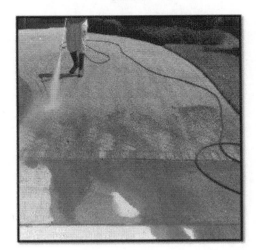 

Outdoor cleaning includes sweeping the patio, removing cobwebs, and washing windows. Pressure washing the driveway and as much of the exterior as possible will also enhance the overall view.

Thomas Kyle

Ensure that water features, swimming pool filters and pumps are working well and that the pool is filled with sparkling clean water.

Please pick up pet droppings.

Remember to put special emphasis on the front door area making sure it's clean and well swept.

Indoor Cleaning

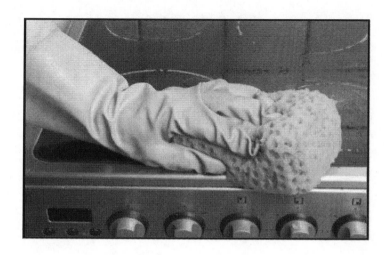

Consider this: Six hours of thorough indoor cleaning by a professional team can elevate the final selling price of the average home by as much as $3,000! The objective of this staging step is to clean and then clean some more, just as you would detail a car.

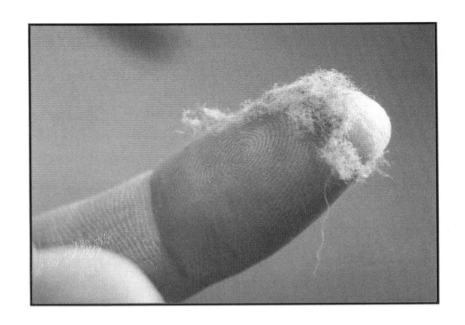

Dirt puts off a buyer faster than anything else.

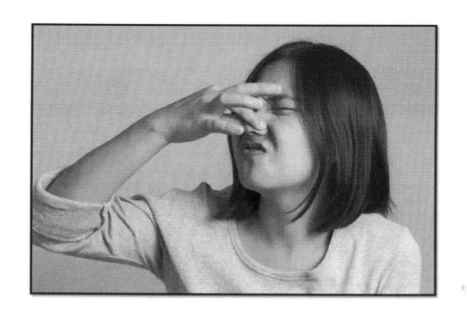

Potential buyers **will** cut short their visit to a home that smells bad. Pet paraphernalia, pet odors, food odors, in fact any odors, are unacceptable. We've come up against cat litter boxes in the kitchen. I call this a "staging boo-boo".

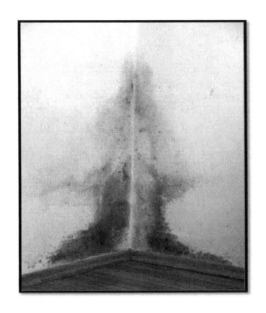

Wage war on dirt and grime and especially bad smells, which may indicate to buyers that there could be bigger problems such as mold or rot. Mold can be a deal-breaker.

Special emphasis must be placed on cleaning areas like floors, carpets, baseboards, electrical outlets, windowsills, light switches and door handles. People will notice lack of cleanliness at eye level, like fireplace mantels and shelves.

Certain cleaning companies offer deep cleaning services where they clean blinds and windows as well as areas already mentioned. My recommendation for doing a deep cleaning would be to call in a professional team, but if you elect to tackle it yourself, here are the areas that need your focus.

If you are not considering replacing carpeting, I suggest professional cleaning. Carpet cleaning is cheap and effective with cleaning companies offering good deals all the time.

If budget is a factor, you could rent a carpet-cleaning machine from the local hardware store or supermarket. At the minimum, I strongly recommend that you vacuum thoroughly.

Remember to clean skylights, windows and window screens. Clean windows definitely affect the brightness of a home, and that's the best light of all – natural light.

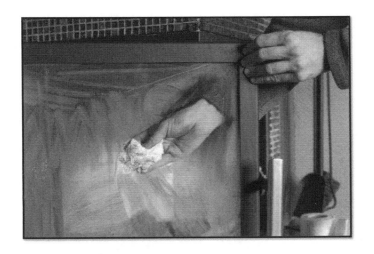

Remember to clean the fireplace. Doors, hinges and window tracks should be cleaned and oiled allowing them to move easily and be squeak free.

Cleaning the kitchen

Your counter tops have been cleared completely and kitchen cabinets are now clutter free. You have eliminated excess kitchen tools, gadgets and expired foodstuffs.

The kitchen must be spotless. If you are doing the cleaning yourself, focus on washing all the surfaces in the kitchen including the interior and exterior of appliances. These need to be odor free and in good working order.

Organize by grouping similar items together as you repack them. Prospective buyers will open cupboards and drawers, so we want them to look organized and clean. Remember to clean knobs and drawer pulls, light fixtures and window coverings.

Use our non-toxic 'power cleaner' in the recipe section to wipe down the interior and exterior of all cabinets, storage cupboards, drawers, refrigerator, freezer and oven. Empty and clean them all, one by one. Clean the sink and the surrounding area as well as any splatters on the walls. Polish all chrome surfaces. Finally, spot clean stains, sweep and then mop the floor and wash the rugs.

There should be no smell of food or anything else in the kitchen. Please avoid the old trick of a bowl of vanilla essence "baking" in a warm oven, unless you plan to produce a plate of cookies. The best smell you can have is the smell of fresh air and that means no smell at all.

And while we're on the subject of smell... If there is a persistent unpleasant odor in the home, you need to get to the root of the problem. If you're dealing with pungent household odors you might need to resort to stronger tactics such as ionizers.

Search the internet for a non-toxic, eco-friendly "bomb" that eliminates serious odors. We strongly discourage the artificial smell of air fresheners and "plug ins" as people may wonder if they are being used to disguise something sinister like mold or damp. We also suggest you avoid the smell of potpourri. In fact, avoid any heady, sweet aromas. Many people are sensitive to smell and many people have perfume allergies.

Cleaning the bathroom

Once all bathroom surfaces have been cleared and updated, this is another area where there is value in having a professional cleaning team. However, if you choose to do it yourself gather the appropriate cleaning materials, put on your rubber gloves and muster up some elbow grease.

Take it from the top. Begin with the fan vent, showerhead, mirrors, shower doors, counter tops and sinks. If necessary, you can use a toothbrush to clean grout and all the places that are hard to reach.

See recipe section at the end of the book for a solution to remove hard water deposits. Throw the shower curtain into the washing machine. Pour a cup of baking soda into the toilet bowl, and let it sit for ten minutes then brush and flush. Finally, sweep and clean the floor.

It is imperative to make sure that the air in the bathroom is fresh, clean and odorless. I prefer the use of all natural essential oils. These can be purchased at any pharmacy or health food store. I specifically recommend the use of citrus oils like lemon or grapefruit because they have a fresh clean smell.

Refer to the **CLEANING CHECKLIST** at the end of the book.

Making a deal with the kids

Let's face it – the hardest part of keeping a staged room clean and tidy (especially kids' bathrooms, bedrooms and the den), is gaining the cooperation of the kids who live in the home while it is being sold.

It's a lot easier for adults to understand the importance of staging, and the importance of maintaining the "staged look" for the duration of the process of the sale.

We have a tried and true method that involves meeting with the whole family to get everyone involved in the home staging process. It involves "serious" negotiations with the children living in the home. It could even include the completion and signing of an informal agreement.

At this meeting you will demonstrate exactly how the staged bathroom should look. You could also provide a photograph of the room so that each day when the kids leave the house for school, they have an exact idea of how the room should be left.

You would be wise to provide a clear checklist of exactly what needs to be done.

For example:

• Flush the toilet and close the lid.

• Dry and wipe off the countertop.

• Pack away your toothbrush and toothpaste, washcloth and towels and replace with "staging accessories" (which should be made easily accessible to the child).

• Make your beds.

• Pack away all your toys, clothes and shoes.

• Put your dirty clothing in the clothes hamper.

Have the kids sign the agreement to keep this "staging assistance" up until the sale of the home is final. They need to understand that there are no half measures.

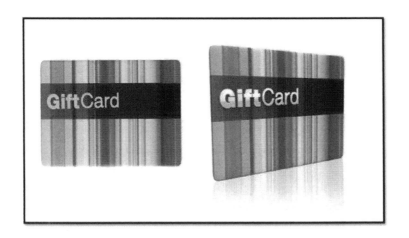

Perhaps you could even offer a 'reward' for a job well done. Having completed four of the five steps, your home will be looking in tip-top condition with all the updating, repairs and cleaning you've done. Now we have just one final step to go, and this is the 'fun' part. Step 5 is all about **DECORATING** your home to sell.

INTERNATIONAL
SCHOOL OF STAGING

STEP 5: DECORATE

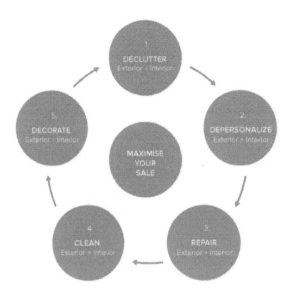

Now let's get on with the final step - DECORATING the house to sell it.

Before   After

Decorating and adding the finishing touches are final steps of staging a home. We market and merchandise the house in such a way that it appeals to the broadest possible pool of buyers. As we enter the property we aim to provide a pleasant journey from the curb to the front door.

Adding seasonal color to flower beds as well as hanging baskets will enhance the exterior appearance of the home.

Before

After

Entertaining in the backyard is always a favorite pastime, so create an inviting alfresco entertainment vignette' by adding a table, chairs and perhaps even an umbrella.

Flank the front door with matching planters filled with vibrant seasonal color. The symmetry will add impact, as will a new front door mat. A potential love affair begins the minute a prospective buyer enters a show house. Create a grand entrance to welcome buyers into the home. People decide within two minutes if they like a residence.

It is imperative that we seize this moment and seduce the house hunter with a perfect setting. The entryway sets the precedent for the rest of the home. Just as we place emphasis on the front door area on the outside, we should give the same care and attention to the entryway.

Adding a mirror on the wall will add to the feeling of size and light, even in the smallest space. Hang mirrors at the eye level of the average person. Space permitting, this is a good place for an entry table or a chest, and perhaps even a chair or two.

This is the perfect opportunity to show a spectacular piece of art and wow visitors with a fabulous fragrant floral arrangement or another display of nature.

As we proceed through the home, we aim to create an atmosphere that is cozy and inviting. The shades and blinds are wide open so as to allow natural light to come in. If the view from a window is unsightly, slant the blinds to block the view, but still allow some natural light into the space. Your home needs to look the very best it possibly can.

Rather than show a vacant home create a vignette in each room using an item of furniture and a few accessories that clearly indicate the function of each room. This is an opportunity to get really creative by using what you already have.

In the living room, we aim to build 'picture perfect' vignettes and create a fantasy for prospective buyers so that they can imagine themselves living in your home.

This will also indicate to house hunters where they might place their furniture.

If your furniture is old and worn or has been mauled by pets, furniture rental or slipcovers are the perfect solutions. Select light, neutral colored fabric slipcovers to cover the larger furniture pieces. These are available online as well as from all of the big stores that sell home goods.

Keep traffic flow open, by 'floating' seating in the center of the room around a coffee table rather than positioning it up against the walls. Try to leave at least 16 to 18 inches of legroom between the coffee table and the chairs or sofa.

If you're renting furniture select pieces that are appropriate for the size and style of your home. Keep in mind the importance of scale so as not to select furniture that is too large for the space. Furniture that is too large will make your rooms look small. Less is best.

Introduce color by using wall art, accessories, throw pillows and throws. Keep the look simple and uncluttered.

Before

After

Mirrors will add light and life to the living room.

When staging your home keep collections to a stylish minimum having packed away anything that is smaller than your hand.

Add a touch of nature to every room. Consider organic materials like driftwood or even large leaves in vases.

The simplest flower arrangement, like a single rose in a bud vase becomes a beautiful focal point.

Create vignettes by grouping accessories in odd numbers – one, three and five object groupings look best.

Vary the sizes and textures of the pieces your group. Juxtapose old and new, light and dark, smooth and rough, formal and casual.

A fireplace is a great focal point. Fill it with logs, pinecones or candles. A shiny set of fireplace tools and screen will complete the picture.

Add additional light with standing lamps and freestanding spotlights positioned behind furniture.

Accessorize the coffee table with stylish coffee table books or trendy magazines, a pretty bowl or some interesting boxes.

A formal dining room presents the perfect opportunity to create memories. Rather than clutter the space with table settings, display candles in candlesticks, a bold centerpiece or a seasonal floral display on a great looking table runner. If the table is old and worn, cover it with a crisp white tablecloth.

Before   After

With the contents of the bedrooms reduced, the focal point is the bed, so if you displayed nothing else other than a neatly made bed with side tables and attractive lamps that would be sufficient.

Instead of renting a bed a double volume aero bed would suffice. Cover the bed with beautiful bed linen and create a headboard with large continental pillows.

Before   After

If your bed linen is dated or faded this would be the ideal opportunity to update your bedroom with some gorgeous new bedding. At the same time, consider buying a set of luxurious white towels. Using these new items to stage your home while you sell it would lessen your to do list when you move into your new home.

Master bedrooms show best in light neutral hues, while kids' rooms can be whimsical in style and brighter in color.

Before   After

A simple display of kids' toys or stuffed animals will clearly indicate the purpose of the room. For added light and ambiance bedside lamps should be left on.

We accessorize the immaculately clean bathroom using stylish and appropriate accessories, which include a pretty tissue box, candles, spa-like bath products and beautiful soaps in their original wrapping. Lay out the accessories in a tight little grouping of odd numbers close together.

I love the color white in a bathroom because it adds to the feeling of cleanliness, newness and luxury.

Adding a white shower curtain, new white, fluffy bath towels would look great. Leave the soap in its original wrapping.

Keep in mind that the kitchen is the most expensive and the most used room in the home. Onto scrupulously clean and bare kitchen counters place only a few bold, colorful and stylish kitchen accessories.

Create impact with a beautiful bowl or basket filled with one variety of fruit like lemons, limes or pears, a lovely recipe book on a stand, some stylish canisters or a gorgeous cookie jar.

Lots of hard work has gone into preparing your home. If you've followed these steps, I imagine your home looks pretty fantastic. This, together with pricing it right will have you off to a great start. Once the final step of decorating the home has been completed, quality professional photographs of both the exterior and the interior should be taken.

Today most house hunting takes place online. Most importantly, throughout the duration of the 'for sale' period do your best to maintain the amazing look you've worked so hard to create. And so we set the stage for a purchase agreement to be signed.

Refer to the **DECORATING CHECKLIST** at the end of the book.

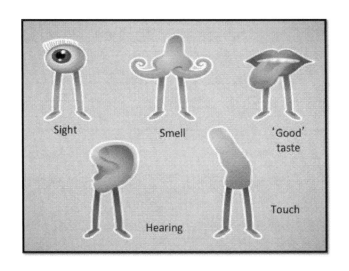

Sight

Smell

'Good' taste

Hearing

Touch

When your house goes 'live' on the market and as you prepare for your open house, there is a great way of doing a final 'check through' by using the five senses.

Sight

Does your home look clean and tidy? Does each room have a clear purpose and identity?

Feel

Is the temperature inside the home 'just right' and comfortable for the season?

Smell

How does your home smell? Is it fresh and clean?

Sound

Would adding some music, like smooth jazz or light classical music make the home seem more inviting?

Taste

Is your home presented in good taste? We wouldn't want to offend potential buyers!

Refer to the **OPEN HOUSE CHECKLIST** prior to your open house.

Well done! You've taken all the necessary steps to show your home off in its best possible light. It has been a real pleasure sharing my passion for home staging with you. I hope that you stay true to these five steps as you prepare your home for the market. I've seen many sellers exceed their asking price by following my action plan. Best wishes to you on your next journey!

John D'urso of Washington stated, "We followed your advice, and our home sold this weekend. We were so pleased with the advice you gave us."

INTERNATIONAL
SCHOOL OF STAGING

www.InternationalSchoolOfStaging.com

CHECKLISTS
DECLUTTER CHECKLIST

DECLUTTER: Outdoor

Δ Shovel snow & de-ice sidewalk.

Δ Organize trash-bin area.

Δ Pick up litter and stack firewood neatly.

Δ Store garden items, sports equipment, and toys.

Δ Trim shrubs.

Δ Prune trees.

Δ Rake leaves.

△ Mow lawn.

FRONT DOOR AREA

△ Remove dusty old and dated wreaths and holiday décor.

DECLUTTER: Indoor

△ Remove dead indoor plants and flowers.

△ Remove small rugs, shoes and sports equipment.

△ Make the beds.

△ Remove all clutter and small appliances from kitchen countertops

△ Store or pack personal items.

Δ Remove personal items

Δ Declutter/clean and organize kitchen cabinets and drawers.

Δ Declutter/clean/organize bathroom cabinets.

Δ Reduce the contents in the garage. Tidy & organize using the five-pile concept.

DEPERSONALISE CHECKLIST

DEPERSONALIZE: Outdoor

Δ Remove "Beware of Dog" and any other signs.

Δ Limit holiday decorations.

Δ Remove pest & rodent exterminating products from storage or garage.

Δ Store recreational vehicles offsite.

Δ Dispose of hazardous waste responsibly www.epa.gov

DEPERSONALIZE: Indoor

Δ Limit holiday decorations.

Δ Remove pets and their food, litter boxes and toys.

Δ Family photographs

Δ Information on the bulletin board

Δ Family calendar and message boards

Δ Refrigerator magnets

Δ Bank and credit card statements

Δ Pin numbers and security codes

Δ Diplomas, awards, certificates

Δ Sports trophies

Δ House and house keys

Δ Weapons

Δ Expensive jewelry

Δ Prescription drugs

Δ Religious items

Δ Hunting memorabilia

Δ Flags of foreign countries

Δ Expensive art objects

Δ Risqué art

Δ Adult literature & personal items

Δ Political literature

Δ Pets, cages and crates

Δ Laptops

Δ Potpourri, perfumed plugins, scented candles

Δ Pet droppings

REPAIR CHECKLIST

REPAIR: Outdoor

Δ Make sure address number is clearly visible.

Δ Paint or replace mailbox.

Δ Make sure outside lights are in good working condition.

Δ Replace missing shingles and roof tiles.

Δ Paint/stain exterior, trim, frames and shutters and decks.

Δ Paint/stain the garage door (replace if necessary).

Δ Make sure sprinkler system is in good working condition.

Δ Make sure swimming pool filter is in good working condition.

Δ Paint and repair gutters and downspouts.

Δ Green the grass using a natural fertilizer.

Δ Replace old storm doors.

Δ Replace damaged or missing bricks and tiles.

Δ Repaint or stain the front door and doorframe.

Δ Oil the hinges to make all doors "squeak-free."

Δ Oil door and window tracks so that they run smoothly.

Δ Polish or replace the front door hardware.

Δ Make sure the key turns easily in the front door lock.

REPAIR: Indoor

Δ Remove if unsightly, or repair or clean window coverings.

Δ Repair cracks in walls and ceilings.

Δ Check smoke and burglar alarms.

Δ Replace and upgrade fixtures wherever possible.

Δ If necessary, repaint walls and ceilings a light neutral color.

Δ Repair and replace all broken items in the kitchen & bathrooms.

Δ Remove & re-grout dirty grout around tiles.

Δ Make sure grout is immaculate.

Δ Remove mildew around bathtub/sinks by removing caulking, cleaning and re-caulking.

Δ Make sure drains are clean and free flowing. .

Δ Repair leaky faucets in the kitchen and bathrooms.

Δ Make sure toilets are in good working order.

Δ Replace and upgrade bathroom hardware/fixtures if possible.

Δ Replace discolored/broken toilet seats.

Δ Ensure the attic is well illuminated.

CLEANING CHECKLIST

CLEAN: Outdoor

Δ Pick up pet droppings.

Δ Clean outside lighting fixtures.

Δ Remove mildew or moss from walls or walks.

Δ Wash windows inside and out.

Δ Sweep and pressure-wash driveways & decks.

Δ Pressure-wash eaves and siding.

Δ Fill swimming pool & water features with clean water.

Δ Sweep the front porch, remove cobwebs and replace the doormat.

Δ Make sure the front doorbell is clean and in good working condition.

CLEAN: Indoor

Δ Empty trashcans, recycle bins, and ashtrays.

Δ Clean fireplace (and fill with pinecones or logs.

Δ Clean carpets, walls, electrical outlets, switch plates, floors, and baseboards.

Δ Clean windows, skylights, window coverings and windowsills.

Δ Clear entry closet (and minimize contents).

Δ Clean door and window runners (and oil to function well).

Δ Polish any visible silver chrome or metal fixtures.

Δ Clean sinks and polish bathroom hardware.

Δ Clean and vacuum carpets throughout the home, behind furniture.

KITCHEN

Δ Wipe down countertops and cabinets.

Δ Clean face of appliances (dishwasher, refrigerator, microwave, dishwasher and oven door)

Δ Wipe down cook top.

Δ Clean inside of microwave.

Δ Clean or replace stove drip pans.

Δ Clean stove knobs, drawer pulls, and light fixtures

Δ Clean window coverings.

Δ Polish all chrome surfaces.

Δ Clean inside and around sink.

Δ Sweep and mop floor.

Δ Clean Baseboards.

Δ Make sure all appliances work well and are clean inside and out.

Δ Eliminate mold – see recipe.

BATHROOM

Δ Make sure bathrooms are scrupulously clean and smell fresh.

Δ Rinse off walls of tub/shower and dry with cloth.

Δ Remove rugs, wastebasket, soap scraps, shampoo bottles.

Δ Clean grout with a toothbrush and grout cleaner. (see recipe)

Δ Clean shower rack and soap dishes.

Δ Clean shower track.

Δ Vanity: spray tile and grout cleaner in sink, soap dish.

Δ Spray countertop with all-purpose cleaner.

Δ Scrub sink.

Δ Use grout brush around the faucet and drain.

Δ Rinse the sink and your rag.

Δ Wipe the vanity countertop.

Δ Wipe down cabinet fronts.

Δ Clean mirror: spray glass cleaner on soft cloth and buff.

Δ Shine the faucets.

Δ Wash the floor and dry the floor.

Δ Replace rugs, bath mat and wastebaskets.

WINDOWS

Δ Clean window screens outdoors with our all-purpose power cleaner and a hose and pat dry.

Δ Vacuum and clean window and door tracks then oil them with WD40.

DECORATING CHECKLIST

DECORATE: Outdoor

Δ Replace or spread wood bark in beds.

Δ Eliminate weeds in cracks. (use white vinegar)

Δ Plant flowerbeds with seasonal color.

Δ Add handing baskets with seasonal color.

Δ Flank the front door with flowerpots of seasonal color.

Δ Rearrange outdoor furniture to create an entertainment vignette.

Δ Illuminate the front door area at night.

DECORATE: Indoor

Δ Consider lighting a fire in cold weather.

Δ Rooms should be well lit, airy and warm.

Δ Open window coverings and turn on lamps.

Δ Hang artwork at eye level.

Δ Have light background music playing.

Δ Display good-quality and spa-like accessories in the bathrooms.

Δ A new white shower curtain, new white towels and bathmat are inexpensive decorations that can be taken with you to your new home.

Δ Accessorize with just a few bold, colorful, stylish pieces.

Δ Set up vignettes that create a fantasy in every room.

The Open House Checklist

Δ Shake off the front door mat.

Δ Sweep the front door area.

Δ Water the planters.

Δ Turn on all the lamps.

Δ Make the beds.

Δ Open the drapes.

Δ Freshen up flower arrangements.

Δ Wipe down bathroom sinks.

Δ Display staging towels.

Δ Close the toilet seat.

Δ Wipe down mirrors.

Δ Wipe down faucets.

Δ Ensure that the toilet bowl is clean.

Δ Empty trash.

Δ Squeegee the shower doors.

Δ Straighten the bath mats.

Δ Wipe down kitchen sinks.

Δ Clean stovetops and counters.

Δ Sweep and mop floors.

Δ Remove pets, pet litter boxes, pet toys, pet food bowls and pet waste from the yard.

Δ Empty garbage.

Δ Throw a lemon down the garbage disposal.

Δ Cookies & lemonade will add a thoughtful touch.

Kids' checklist

You would need to create your own kids checklist, for example:

• Flush the toilet and close the lid.

• Dry and wipe off the countertop.

• Pack away your toothbrush and toothpaste, washcloth and towels – and replace with "staging accessories" (which should be made easily accessible to the child).

• Make your bed.

• Pack away all your toys, clothes and shoes.

• Put your dirty clothing in the clothes hamper.

100% NON-TOXIC ECO-FRIENDLY RECIPES

Formulated for reduced environmental impact

<u>WEED KILLER</u>

Ingredients:

1 Gallon Vinegar

2 Cups Epson Salt

1/4 Cup Blue Dawn Dish Soap

Mix together and spray:

Wait for a day ....

Safer than Roundup

ALTERNATIVE WEED KILLER

Straight white vinegar

ANOTHER WEED KILLER

Boiling water

SIDEWALK DE-ICER

For icy steps and sidewalks in freezing temperatures, mix together:

1 teaspoon of Dawn dishwashing liquid,

1 tablespoon of rubbing alcohol

1/2 gallon hot water

Pour over walkways. They will not refreeze.

De-icing Salt is bad for the environment as well as dog paws.

DRIVEWAY CLEANER

If you motor oil stains on your driveway, use kitty litter to clean up the excess oil and then use a scrubbing brush with a solution of biodegradable Dawn dishwashing detergent with warm water to safely and effectively remove excess motor oil.

POOL CLEANING

For a sparkling clean swimming pool, squirt Dawn down the middle of the pool. It will attract all the dirt, suntan oils and debris and will move to the edges of the pool for easy clean up!

DRAIN CLEANER

Pour a cup of baking soda and a cup of salt down the drain, followed by 3 cups of white vinegar. Let it stand a few minutes, then flush with a pot of boiling water.

NON TOXIC DRAINO

1 Cup salt

1 Cup baking soda

1 Cup vinegar - 1 cup boiling water

Leave to sit for 15 minutes –

Follow up by pouring through a large pot of boiling water

Empty the sink. Pour one cup of baking soda followed by one cup of table salt and then pour a cup of white vinegar. Wait for ten minutes and flush it with a large pot of boiling water. Flush with lots of hot running water

DE-GRIME PATIO FURNITURE

Add a squirt of dish detergent to a bowl of warm water.

Use the mixture to wipe down your outdoor tables and chairs.

Rinse clean with the garden hose.

TO CLEAN PATIO CUSHIONS

Scrub with a stiff brush dipped in white vinegar.

Scrub stubborn stains with baking soda on a wet sponge

TO REMOVE THE ODOR OF CIGARETTE SMOKE

Household odors are a tough fix. First make sure that all fabrics in the room have been cleaned (including curtains, upholstery, cushions and carpeting).

Then, leave bowls of vinegar around the room to absorb any leftover smoke. Encourage any smokers to smoke outdoors while their house is on the market.

You may need to resort to renting an ionizer

AIR FRESHENER

Fill a spray bottle with 1/2 cup of water and add 30 drops of essential oil. We specifically recommend the use of citrus oils like lemon, or grapefruit. Spray this solution into the air to add freshness to a room or closet. Lemon and grapefruit essential oils can add a fresh, natural scent to an already clean home.

WINDOW CLEANER

Mix 3 drops of blue Dawn in 1 gallon water with 1 cup of white vinegar. Fill a spray bottle with the solution. Use the same as a window cleaner.

REMOVING DECALS

Sponge vinegar on any decals that stubbornly resist removal.

Leave for 10 minutes and scrape them off using credit card to avoid scratching the surface

TO REMOVE PAINT FROM GLASS

Heat white vinegar until lukewarm and apply with a nylon scrubber.

TO REMOVE WALLPAPER

Pour a cup of white vinegar into two gallons of hot water, and then transfer that into a spray bottle. Apply to wallpaper until very wet. Let stand about 15 minutes or until wallpaper is loose.

VINEGAR

Straight white vinegar is an environmentally friendly and powerful 'all-in-one' household cleaner that can be used on virtually any surface in the house -- except for materials such as marble and limestone. It is easily diluted with water, inexpensive, and kills 99 percent of bacteria, 82 percent of mold and 80 percent of germs and viruses. We use Vinegar to clean mirrors, glass, tile, stainless steel and chrome.

ANT REPELLANT

Wipe countertops with vinegar.

ANT REPELLANT

We use this nontoxic formula to banish ants. Dip a Q-tip into cinnamon essential oil. Find the source of the pathway where the ants originate. Draw a line across the path that the ants are travelling – it will create a barrier that the ants won't cross.

REPEL HOUSEPLANT INSECTS

A safe, effective insect repellant for Aphids and Spider mites

Put a drop of Dawn Dishwashing Liquid in a spray bottle, fill the rest of the bottle with water, shake well, and mist your household plants with the soapy water.

TO REMOVE SCUFFS FROM VINYL FLOORING

Put a little baking soda on a damp sponge. Use a little elbow grease the scuffs will disappear.

TO REMOVE CRAYON MARKS

From washable walls and floors, gently scrub with baking soda on a damp sponge or nylon scrubber.

Use baking soda to absorb spilled oil and grease. Then wet the area and scour it with a nylon scrubber.

USE AN IRON TO REMOVE CARPET STAINS

Mix 1 cup vinegar with 2 cups water in a spray bottle and douse the stain with the mixture. Then, place a damp cloth over the stain. Use the steam setting on the iron and iron the spot for about 30 seconds. For seriously tough stains, repeat the steps.

ECO FRIENDLY HERBAL CARPET FRESHENER

Ingredients:

1/2 cup dried and finely crushed dried lavender flowers

1/2 cup dried and finely crushed rosemary leaves

1 cup baking soda

Combine all the ingredients in a large container with a tight- fitting lid. Shake very well to blend. Sprinkle the mixture liberally (but not thickly) on your carpet and let it sit for an hour or so, and then vacuum. It will neutralize carpet odors and give the room a pleasant smell that will last for days

MOLD

Spray undiluted Hydrogen Peroxide on the mold, leave for 10 minutes, Scrub off – use 3% concentration solution that you buy from your pharmacy.

ANOTHER MOLD FIGHTING RECIPE

1 cup distilled vinegar

20 drops tea tree oil

REMOVING PERMANENT MARKER

Use a few drops of lemon essential oil and a good dose of elbow grease.

Non Toxic 'POWER CLEANER' for all surfaces including Glass

2 Cups Water

1 Cup blue Dawn Dishwashing Liquid

1 Cup Vinegar

Mixed together.

CLEANING FLOORS

Ceramic Tiles – (see Non-toxic power cleaner)

Wooden Floors – 1 Cup Vinegar to 2 gallons of water in a bucket

To clean Vinyl & Linoleum Floors – use non toxic power cleaner

CLEANING GREASY RESIDUE OFF KITCHEN CABINETS

Ingredients:

½ Cup vegetable oil

1 Cup baking soda

40 drops lemon essential oil

Mix these 3 ingredients together with a spoon. Using a sponge, cloth and an old toothbrush, apply the paste to the cabinet doors in light circular movements

Wipe off the mixture with a damp cloth.

CLEANING GAS STOVE BURNERS

Place the burners in separate gallon size Ziploc bag, along with 2-3 tablespoons of ammonia.

Do not puncture the bag. Leave to soak for 12 hours before rinsing

CLEANING YOUR OVEN

Ingredients:

Water

Spray bottle

Baking soda

A scouring sponge

Vinegar

A small bowl

1. Remove the oven racks.

2. Mix a couple of spoonsful of baking soda with some water in the bowl. Create a paste that will be easily spread on oven surfaces.

3. Spread the paste on the inside of the oven (baking soda will turn brown). Let it sit overnight (at least 12 hours).

4. The next day, take a wet rag and wipe out as much of the baking soda paste as you can.

5. Put some vinegar in a spray bottle and spritz on surfaces where you still see baking soda residue. Then wipe with a wet rag.

6. Put the racks back in the oven and turn the oven onto a very low temperature for 15-20 minutes to let dry.

CLEANING THE OVEN WINDOW

1 Make a paste out of baking soda and water.

2 Apply the paste directly to the window and let it sit for 30 minutes.

3 Use a clean rag to wipe the window clean.

CLEANING THE MICROWAVE

Clean the microwave by heating a cup of water and a chopped-up lemon on high until the microwave's window is steamy. Leave the bowl sit for 15 minutes before you open the door. Cleans really nicely after a kind of sauna for microwaves.

CLEANING THE DISHWASHER

Fill 2 coffee mugs with white vinegar and stand them upright in an empty dishwasher, 1 on the top shelf and one on the bottom shelf. Pour an extra cup of vinegar into the machine.

 Run a hot cycle.

REMOVING HARD WATER STAINS (the chalky sediment that collects around the kitchen faucet)

Ingredients and method:

1. Put 2 cups of distilled white vinegar in a spray bottle

2. Add in 1/4 cup of lemon juice.

3. Fill the majority of the remaining space of the spray bottle with blue Dawn soap

 4. Shake the bottle to mix together ingredients.

Use for hard water stains. Spray it on liberally and let it sit for 30 minutes. Then scrub away the grime. Rinse and dry.

HOW TO MAKE STAINLESS STEEL APPLIANCES SHINE

Clean stainless steel panels using a damp microfiber cloth. Dry using another clean, dry microfiber cloth. Apply thin coat of olive oil and polish to shine

ANOTHER WAY TO MAKE STAINLESS STEEL SHINE

1 cup of baking soda

1/4 cup of lemon juice

3 TBS Borax

Water

Mix together the first 3 ingredients into a medium bowl.

Add enough water into the mixture to create a thick paste.

Dip a clean rag into the paste and rub directly on your stainless steel appliances.

Gently wipe the paste off with a clean wet rag.

UNCLOG A TOILET WITHOUT A PLUNGER

A cup of Dawn detergent poured into a clogged toilet allowed to sit for 20 minutes and then followed with a bucket of hot water poured from waist height will clear out the toilet.

TOILET CLEANER

Pour 1 Cup Baking Soda into the toilet bowl, add 20 drops lemon or grapefruit essential oil. Then finally add a cup of vinegar. When the mixture begins to fizz, use a toilet brush and some elbow grease and scrub the toilet bowl.

TUB AND SHOWER CLEANER

Take a spray bottle and fill it halfway with white vinegar. Heat the mixture in the microwave. Fill the rest of the way with blue Dawn. Put lid on and shake to mix well. Spray on your tub and shower walls. Leave to rest for a few minutes then rinse off.

BATHTUB CLEANER

¾ cup baking soda

¼ Cup Dr Bronners peppermint soap

2 Tablespoons Water

Mix a paste inside a bowl using the 3 ingredients. Use on sponge or cloth to clean bathtub.

SHOWER FLOOR CLEANER

Clean a stained shower floors with a coating of blue Dawn. Leave to sit overnight.

Scrub with a stiff brush.

GROUT CLEANER

I have 2 great recipes for cleaning grout.

1. Use a mixture of equal quantities of vinegar and water. Wash over the tile and grout with a sponge

2. Pour a thin stream of Hydrogen Peroxide over the grout. Use a toothbrush dipped in baking soda and scrub the grout.

ANOTHER GROUT CLEANING IDEA

Blue Dawn or even toothpaste with a toothbrush or scrubbing brush and scrub.

REPEL ANTS

Spray counter-tops, cupboards or any other area where you have a problem with ants, using a solution of 1 cup Dawn and 1 cup water. Wipe dry. Residue that remains will repel ants.

PAINT OR GREASE REMOVER FOR HANDS

Dawn combined with vegetable oil makes for the perfect paint or grease remover. Simply combine a little bit of both in your hands then rub it over affected areas. The corn oil and the dishwashing liquid both help to dissolve the grease and paint.

WOOD POLISH

Mix 1 cup of olive oil

¼ cup of white vinegar

20 drops of lemon essential oil

Put into a spray bottle for your own DIY furniture polish.

LEATHER FURNITURE CLEANER

Use a good quality wax shoe polish to remove scratches and scuffs from leather couches.

THE END

ACKNOWLEDGEMENTS

Special thanks to:

My beloved husband Marc, and my precious sons Robbie & Ricky Capelluto

Chris Angell – my coach

Jill Levy - editor

Mae Boettcher – designed the cover

Michele Fritzler & Mona Renner, both students whom I've mentored and who have allowed me to feature their work in this book

ONE LAST THING...

If you enjoyed this book or found it useful I'd be very grateful if you'd post a short review on Amazon. Your support really does make a difference.

I read all the reviews personally so I can get your feedback and make this book even better.

Thanks again for your support!

Andy Capelluto

Made in the USA
San Bernardino, CA
11 December 2016